Original title:
Life's Questions and My Disastrous Answers

Copyright © 2025 Creative Arts Management OÜ
All rights reserved.

Author: Levi Montgomery
ISBN HARDBACK: 978-1-80566-181-8
ISBN PAPERBACK: 978-1-80566-476-5

Whispers of Uncertainty

In the mirror, I see my face,
Wondering if I'm out of place.
Did I leave the stove on today?
Or is it just my mind at play?

I seek advice from my pet cat,
He stares back, gives nary a chat.
Should I trust a sock on the floor?
Or ask the shoe where it's been before?

An Odyssey of Second Guesses

In the quest for wisdom, I took a leap,
But tripped on my thoughts, it's a perilous sweep.
Found answers in pockets, oh what a sight,
Only to realize they escaped in the night.

Maps all around me, directions unclear,
I asked the goldfish, it coughed up a tear.
Confusion like weather, a storm on the way,
Yet here I am laughing, come join the display.

Illusions of Certainty

I thought I had it figured, a plan in my hand,
But my GPS broke, now I'm lost in the sand.
Wrote down some rules, they crumbled like dust,
It's hard to have certainty when nothing's robust.

I fluffed up my answers, made them all neat,
But they danced like balloons, took off in the heat.
I try to be savvy, play it so cool,
Yet slip on a banana peel, grandpa's old school.

Answers that Evaporate

I caught a few answers like flies in the air,
But they buzzed away, like they didn't care.
Questions piled high, like laundry on floor,
I folded my guesses, but they wanted to soar.

Every time I ask, the answers sneak off,
Like cats in the night, they're too sly to scoff.
With humor, I chase them, give it my all,
But they vanish like socks in the laundry's dull haul.

The Tides of Confusion

Riding the waves of a cerebral sea,
I surf on confusion, it's just so free.
Thoughts drift like driftwood, no anchor in sight,
As I paddle for answers, I'm swallowed by fright.

The compass is spinning, it's lost all its charm,
I chuckle at chaos, it seems to disarm.
Questions are deep, like the ocean's own bed,
I float on my folly, just follow my head.

Chasing Shadows of Understanding

I chased a thought, it ran so fast,
I tripped on wisdom, what a blast.
The answers danced just out of reach,
I laughed so hard, they taught me speech.

A friend once asked, "What's life all about?"
I mumbled something, then just shouted.
He rolled his eyes, said, "Try again,"
But I just giggled—where's the zen?

In books and dreams, I search for clues,
Yet every page seems full of blues.
I scribbled diagrams, none made sense,
Turns out, fun is the best expense.

So here I stand, a merry fool,
With questions wide and playful tool.
I'll chase these shadows with bright delight,
And twirl in laughter till the night.

The Unasked and Unanswered

I pondered hard what should I ask,
Yet somehow found it quite a task.
The universe shrugged, as I sighed,
   I guess it's fine to just abide.

At dinner parties, folks discuss,
The meaning of it all—no fuss.
I nod my head, though clueless still,
   I wish for snacks to fill that thrill.

The hitchhiker raised his thumb with glee,
   He asked for answers—who'd agree?
   I offered chips instead of gold,
He bit and laughed, our souls consoled.

So ask away, but not too loud,
The silence might attract a crowd.
Let's revel in the silly dance,
And let the questions take their chance!

Beneath the Weight of Choices

I stood before a shelf so vast,
Should I choose cookies or a repast?
The scales tipped with a crumbly treat,
I grinned and said, "This can't be beat."

In life, they say, we must decide,
But what if choices slip and slide?
I wore two hats, then five or more,
Confusion ruled; I fell on the floor.

A voice said, "Pick the path that shines,"
But all the roads looked torn like vines.
I ended up at a random fair,
With cotton candy in my hair.

So here I stand, with arms full wide,
And choices made that won't abide.
Let's laugh at fate as it prances near,
For every laugh dissolves a fear.

Labyrinths of the Soul

I wandered through a maze so deep,
With walls of thoughts that made me weep.
Each corner turned a different way,
With signs that read, "Enjoy the fray."

A parrot perched said, "Stop and chat,"
I asked him questions—how about that?
He squawked profound wisdom quite in jest,
"Just wing it, kid, it's all a fest!"

In the garden of my swirling mind,
I planted dreams, yet weeds entwined.
Pulled out a thought, and out came snickers,
The universe laughed, it loves the trickers.

So here I roam, in giggles lost,
Each twist and turn, I pay the cost.
I'll dance with shadows, no end in sight,
For humor shines where hearts take flight.

A Canvas of Uncertainty

With colors splashed, my brush goes wild,
Each stroke a guess, like a curious child.
I paint my dreams in shades of doubt,
Only to find they drift about.

Mistakes become my finest art,
A masterpiece crafted with a clumsy heart.
I laugh at messes that seem profound,
In the chaos, joy is always found.

Echoes in the Abyss

I shout my thoughts into the void,
They bounce back; have I been toyed?
My musings echo, oh what a sound,
A riddle wrapped in silence found.

Wisdom whispers, but I can't discern,
As laughter and confusion take their turn.
In the depths of my ponderous quest,
I've learned to giggle at my best guess.

The Journey of Unresolved Thoughts

On a train of ideas, I take a ride,
Stops and starts, nowhere to hide.
Each station holds a thought or two,
Some are silly, some might be true.

The conductor's lost, the map's a joke,
Yet here I sit, and still I poke.
With snacks of doubt and drinks of fear,
I toast to chaos, my thoughts are here.

Whims of the Mind

My mind's a circus, clowns galore,
Thoughts juggling hopes on a tightrope floor.
They tumble and fall, a silly show,
As laughter echoes, the doubts just flow.

I throw confetti of dreams up high,
A parade of wishes that wave goodbye.
Yet in this carnival, joy's my find,
For every flop, a burst of kind.

Inquiries Beneath the Skin

Why is the sky so blue today?
Perhaps it's sad or on holiday.
I asked the tree, it just stood still,
Perhaps I'd better try a hill.

The ants march past, in tidy lines,
Are they lost or looking for signs?
I tried to ask, but they just ran,
Maybe their leader's a wise man.

I ponder deep on toast and jam,
Is breakfast food or a theatrical sham?
The toast replied, with crumbs so bright,
"I'm your muse, your morning delight!"

So here I am, with queries vast,
In a world where answers flee fast.
I laugh at notions I can't define,
And chalk it up to coffee and wine.

The Fragile Threads of Belief

Do ducks wear shoes when they waddle?
In my dreams, they hold a raddle.
I asked a fish its fashion sense,
It just swam off, how very dense!

Around the corner, in a hat shop,
I found a snail, who offered a bop.
"Wear it snug, it won't make you slow!"
I thought, why not? I'll give it a go.

Pages turn in books of sage,
What's wisdom, but a wordy cage?
A cat meowed, "Just bask in the sun,"
I replied, "But I'm the only one!"

So I craft my thoughts like tiny threads,
In the grand tapestry where logic treads.
With every stitch a laugh is spun,
And somehow, I think I'm having fun.

Whispers of Uncertainty

Is it the cat that's plotting strife,
Or is it simply my wobbly knife?
I asked the moon if it could glow,
It chuckled softly, "You already know."

A squirrel inspected acorns with flair,
I wondered if it sensed my despair.
But as it danced, so sprightly and quick,
I felt a tickle—a cosmic trick.

With gnashing teeth and furrowed brow,
I pondered existence and how, oh how,
To run from fate like a sneaky mouse,
Or ask it to join my singing house?

In all the whispers that fill the air,
Absurdity plays, with melodious flair.
I laugh at the riddles that spin my way,
And hope for wisdom with each passing day.

The Riddles I Weave

What's a gnome doing in my yard?
Laughing loudly, it must be hard.
I asked it for answers on matters profound,
It just twirled around and fell to the ground.

The goldfish bubbles, unbothered, serene,
Hints to me about things yet unseen.
"Water's the key!" it whispered with grace,
I replied, "Then where's my happy place?"

Each riddle I weave is a patchwork bright,
Made of nonsense and half-baked insight.
A wise old owl perched high on a tree,
Laughed and hooted, "It's all nonsense, you see!"

So I dance with questions, and quirky surprise,
In this circus of thoughts, adventure lies.
And if I fumble through the cosmic dance,
I'll laugh it off—after all, what's the chance?

Fables of Untraveled Roads

I took a path that looked quite nice,
But tripped over my dreams, oh what a price!
A map in hand, but lost my way,
Turned left at smiles, found shades of gray.

I wandered far, with thoughts so grand,
Met a talking tree, asked for a hand.
It whispered back, with wisdom unclear,
"Just laugh it off; don't shed a tear."

Signs on the Sidewalk

Saw a sign that read 'this way's bliss',
But turned around and fell for the abyss.
Left my clues on crumpled leaves,
Found wisdom in jokes, and a thief.

With every step, I made it worse,
Chasing answers, caught in reverse.
The sidewalk giggled as I tripped,
In a comedy act, I was the script.

The Mirage Beyond the Horizon

Chased a vision over sand and stone,
Thought I'd find gold, just found a drone.
It buzzed around, mocking my stride,
Said, "Check your brain, it's not outside!"

Took a sip from an empty cup,
Promised myself, I'd never give up.
But the sun set low, and shadows danced,
Leaving me alone, in a funny trance.

A Symphony of Missteps

I played a tune on my life's old keys,
But the notes fell flat, caught in the breeze.
Each step a rhythm, a wobbly prance,
Led me to places I wouldn't chance.

Tripped on a high note, slipped on a low,
Signaled the world, 'Hey, don't you know?'
Danced like a fool, and expected applause,
But found only crickets, and slight, playful jaws.

Musings of a Wayward Mind

Why do socks disappear, oh how they flee?
It's like a plot twist in a bad comedy.
I search beneath the couch and in the dark,
Only to find them pilfered by a shark.

Why do I trip on flat, stable ground?
It's like my feet have a mind, quite unbound.
I tumble with flair, a clumsy ballet,
While onlookers chuckle, 'What a display!'

Why does coffee spill when I'm running late?
It's like my cup is plotting my fate.
I fashion my beard a new caffeinated style,
As I wipe it away with an exasperated smile.

Why does my GPS lead me astray?
It's a stealthy game of 'choose your own way.'
I arrive at destinations unplanned,
Wondering if Google has its head in the sand.

Tides of Reflection

Why is my hair so wild and free?
It's like it's auditioning for a tree.
With each gust of wind, it dances with glee,
While I wish for a calm, tame legacy.

Why does my phone think I'm not home?
It texts my fridge and makes it moan.
I whisper sweet nothings into the air,
While my appliances plot my despair.

Why do I think I can cook like a pro?
Last night's stew looked like a horror show.
I dress it with herbs, like a chef with flair,
Yet it turns out like a cautionary tale of despair.

Why does the toast always fall face down?
It must know I wear a perpetual frown.
I pick it up, with a sigh and a shake,
And laugh at the mess I keep trying to make.

Jigsaw Pieces of the Self

Why do my plants seem to join a cult?
With every wilt, they make me feel like an adult.
I water them weekly, but they just stare,
Mocking my efforts with their vacant glare.

Why do I think every puzzle fits right?
I force the wrong piece with all of my might.
It's a masterpiece of wrong, a sight to behold,
Like my attempts at dating, quite tragically bold.

Why do I laugh at jokes no one gets?
It's my quirky charm, filled with regrets.
I relish the silence, it's well worth the wait,
As the crickets my loyal audience celebrate.

Why does my phone have plans of its own?
It sends my messages to places unknown.
As if it's a spy with a secret to tell,
I ponder my gadget fits in my shell.

The Mirror of My Missteps

Why does my reflection shake its head so?
It knows my stumbles, the slips, and the woe.
Every lost shoe and mismatched sock
Echoes in giggles that mock and shock.

Why do I dance like a potato on fire?
When the music plays, I truly aspire.
Yet each twist and turn feels like a feat,
That leaves me wondering if my feet can compete.

Why do I still sing in the shower of dreams?
While the water echoes a cacophony of screams?
I belt out the notes with an opera flair,
Oblivious to neighbors who stop and stare.

Why is my toast always slightly burnt?
Is it my culinary skills that are truly turned?
I play it off cool, a gourmet disaster,
As I feast on the evidence, faint heart beating faster.

Serenade of the Unanswered

Why do birds sing on sunny days?
I asked the cat, who just turned away.
She licked her paw with utmost grace,
And left me pondering in empty space.

Is pie really better than cake?
My mouth said yes, my heart a mistake.
The fork dropped down, a tragic clank,
Behind my laughter, a pie chart sank.

Do unicorns come in shades of gray?
I made a wish, then watched it sway.
In clouds of glitter, the answer hid,
While all I found was a dancing squid.

When Doubt Takes Flight

Should I wear socks with sandals today?
My friends just laughed and walked away.
Is style subjective? Who can tell?
They're probably right; I wish them well.

What's the meaning of a pickle jar?
A wise fish said it's the best by far.
But when opened, my plans did flub,
And I ended up in a sticky hub.

Can a snail really win a race?
I cheered him on, but lost my place.
In the end, with laughter so sly,
I waved goodbye, with a buttered pie.

The Clarity of Chaos

Is cereal a soup? Ah, the strife!
Milk plus crunch, a daily life.
I weighed my thoughts on a spoon so bold,
While my breakfast giggled, uncontrolled.

Is it too late to learn to dance?
The mirror mocked with each missed chance.
While tripping over my two left feet,
I laughed so hard, I lost my seat.

What's the secret to a perfect pie?
A slice of patience? Good luck, oh my!
But dough's a tease, it won't comply,
And my kitchen's now a dessert supply.

The Tempo of Turmoil

Why do shoes go missing at night?
My dog just sighed, he seemed polite.
With mismatched pairs, I marched out brave,
Onlookers giggled; I was their fave.

Can a tree ever feel lonely too?
I asked one once, it rustled — whew!
With leaves that danced in the evening breeze,
It whispered tales of birds and bees.

What's the best joke to tell a frog?
He pondered hard, beneath the fog.
He croaked a pun that made me sigh,
Then jumped away, and left me dry.

Dilemmas at Dawn

Should I rise with the sun?
Or snooze just one more time?
The coffee pot is calling me,
But the bed's a perfect crime.

Pancakes or cereal today?
Decisions weigh on my mind.
Flip a coin, or just guess?
I'm sure chaos will be kind.

The dog needs a morning walk,
Yet my socks refuse to match.
Is that a spider in the corner?
Oh look, it's breakfast time—scratch!

Oh, what a silly start,
With choices piling high.
I'll wear that spiffy hat,
And convince the world I fly.

Unraveled Threads of Thought

Each idea spins like a top,
But I forgot how to stop.
Should I knit a sweater or not?
I think I'll just eat a mop.

How many socks are in this load?
Did I wear this one last week?
Finding answers like a code,
But my brain just feels antique.

Should I sing, or just hum low?
Will they cheer or will they boo?
Join my dance, or let me go?
It's up to you, I guess, woo-hoo!

A fabric patchwork of my mind,
Stitched together with some flair.
Each knot tells a funny tale,
Of tangled truths floating in air.

The Weight of What Ifs

What if I wore polka dots?
Or danced on my living room floor?
I'd surely trip on the cat,
Then I'd tumble right out the door.

What if oatmeal's my best friend?
Or if I joined a circus troupe?
I could juggle breakfast bowls,
And be the clumsy clown on loop.

What if I spoke in rhyme?
Would it drive my folks away?
Or would they join in the fun,
And sprinkle laughter all the way?

Each thought is a heavy brick,
What if I let them fly?
In a world of silly 'what ifs',
I'll laugh until I cry.

Navigating the Labyrinth

In a maze of endless turns,
I follow signs like a fool.
Left, right, or up the wall?
I may just use the pool.

Which path leads me to the cheese?
Or keeps me free from fright?
I'm armed with snacks to bribe,
But the minotaur's not polite.

Webs of choices in my head,
Like spaghetti on a plate.
I'll twirl these thoughts around,
And hope it all is fate.

Oh, wandering in this jest,
Adventure leads to fun abounds.
I might just lose my way,
But laughter's still the best of hounds.

When Curiosity Burns

What's that smell? Is it my thought?
Perhaps it's wisdom, so badly caught.
I ask the stars, they flicker and tease,
While my brain just cooks like a winter cheese.

I sought for truth in a cereal box,
Found a toy instead, shaped like a fox.
Should I trust my gut or my grumbling heart?
Even my socks don't know where to start.

Questions abound like squirrels in trees,
But answers hide like a cold summer breeze.
I'll take a risk, roll the dice of fate,
But the dice just laugh and say, "Wait! Wait!"

So with a grin, I'll wander astray,
Collecting my quirks along the way.
For every stumble is a dance, it seems,
In this circus of life, I follow my dreams.

Fragments of Confusion

Once I pondered if cats wore shoes,
My neighbor chuckled, leaving me bruised.
The universe joked behind my back,
While I sipped tea from a paper stack.

Do ducks get cold on a windy day?
Or do they strut in a feathery sway?
I scribble notes on napkins, my guide,
As reason laughs and takes a joyride.

Do penguins feel love? Or just disdain?
These thoughts are heavy like a weather vane.
I chase my shadows in wild pursuit,
Only to find I'm lost in a suit.

So here I sit, with a fork and a knife,
Trying to carve up bits of my life.
In this puzzle of oddities, I confess,
I might be the center of my own mess.

Answers in Shadows

With each question, I trip on my feet,
In the corner lurks wisdom, ominous and sweet.
I ask the shadows where they've been,
They laugh and whisper, "Lost in your skin."

The sun beams bright, but I stand in gloom,
Searching for answers in a tiny room.
Where do socks go when they disappear?
Maybe they're off, sipping soda and beer!

A wise old turtle once said with a glance,
"Take life lightly; it's just a dance."
But what of the rug? It occasionally trips,
Leaving me sprawled with my unruly quips.

Yet in the chaos, laughter ensues,
Turning my woes into silly news.
For each mistake is a reason to cheer,
And I'll wear my confusion like a chandelier.

The Search for Clarity

I scoured the woods for wisdom's bark,
Chased after thoughts that just missed the mark.
The trees just chuckled, swayed with the breeze,
While squirrels took bets on my search for keys.

I crafted a map with crayons and glue,
But honesty's path turned a shade of blue.
Should I follow my dreams or the pizza place?
My stomach dictates my life at a fast pace.

I ponder at night, on my bed like a boat,
Drifting on wavy ideas that float.
Clarity's shining like a mirage in sand,
I just want answers! But life's out of hand.

In pursuit of the light, I trip and I fall,
But laughter, dear friend, beats answers with gall.
I'll embrace confusion, that slippery art,
As I juggle my questions with a giggling heart.

Echoes of Mistaken Paths

I asked where happiness grows,
But found it in mismatched clothes.
Like socks that wander far apart,
A fashion statement, not an art.

I sought the meaning of true love,
But settled for a shoe-sized shove.
With every heart I tried to catch,
I learned to dodge the awkward match.

What's the secret to success, I said,
And tripped on dreams I left for dead.
But laughter bloomed where fears would creep,
In blunders made, my heart's at peace.

So here's to all the bumbling fun,
My answers wear the light of sun.
Though paths may twist, I felt the game,
Mistakes have often brought me fame.

Puzzles in the Fog

I wondered how to steer my fate,
But followed clouds that looked like cake.
Each choice a slice, half-baked and sweet,
I nibbled crumbs, my favorite treat.

In searching for the greater plan,
I lost myself in a lost-and-found.
Yet every puzzle, every clue,
Was made of laughs and silly dew.

What's the reason for the chase?
I asked a cat who moved with grace.
She winked and purred, then leaped away,
Leaving me to ponder play.

Among the fog, I chased my dream,
But found it tangled like a seam.
Yet in the laughter of the chase,
I found my joy, my happy place.

When Clarity Evades

I reached for wisdom wrapped in gold,
Yet found confusion, crisp and old.
It whispered softly, cracked a joke,
Then hid beneath a pile of smoke.

In pure pursuit of knowledge rare,
I slipped and landed in a chair.
With every thought that spun around,
The clarity just made me drown.

I pondered long but missed the score,
Between the answers and the lore.
And when I thought I'd hit the mark,
The candle flickered, lost the spark.

So here I sit, my head in hands,
With riddles woven by my plans.
But laughter dances in the mess,
A joyful shrug at life's big jest.

The Query and the Quarrel

I asked my mirror who's the best,
It cracked a smile but failed the test.
With every answer tossed around,
The quarrel broke, no victor found.

In seeking truths of heart and mind,
I found the humor, one of a kind.
My questions fluttered like a kite,
But tangling strings brought endless fright.

What's the secret to the stars above?
I asked a dog who's full of love.
He barked in joy and danced in glee,
Claiming wisdom in puppy glee.

So here's to questions, wild and free,
They twist and turn, just let them be.
For every squabble brings a cheer,
And laughter's melody is always near.

Colliding with My Own Reflections

In the mirror, my thoughts collide,
I ask, 'Who's this?' with eyes open wide.
Answers bounce like an echoing sound,
Each reflection is a puzzle unbound.

I ponder deep over tea and toast,
Do I have a brain, or just at most?
The face looks wise, but the mind's a mess,
Oh, what a fun little game of guess!

Should I pursue dreams, or take a nap?
Each choice I make feels like a trap.
The dog looks up like he knows best,
With a wag of the tail, he suggests rest.

Questions rain down, do I need a coat?
Diving into thoughts, I can hardly float.
Falling in laughter, my answers seem grim,
But in this circus, I'm ready to swim.

The Compass Backwards

With a compass pointing due south,
I grinned and opened my mouth.
It said 'North,' but I felt like a clown,
'Travel backwards; let's turn this around!'

Navigating life with a map upside down,
Thoughts take me for a merry-go-round.
Lost in the woods, I look for a snack,
Accidentally following my own track.

Each turn I take is a giggle in vain,
As trees whisper secrets of joy and pain.
Maybe the path is just full of laughs,
Or perhaps it's just my silly mishaps.

So here's to the journey, wherever it leads,
With my backwards compass, planting strange seeds.
In this madcap dance, I'll take all the spins,
Laughing at where the adventure begins.

Stumbling Upon Answers Yet to Be Asked

Stumbled through doors I thought were sealed,
Tripped over thoughts that were never revealed.
Finding answers with a puzzled frown,
Like socks in a dryer, all turned around.

Questions linger like smoke in the air,
While I search my pockets as if they're bare.
Out pops a snack; who knew I would find,
The one missing riddle that bubbles my mind?

Laughter erupts at my own clumsy ways,
Chasing shimmers of wisdom that play.
Every answer I chase turns on its heel,
In this game of confusion, it's surreal.

So here's to the journey of questions unknown,
Where the humorous moments are playfully sown.
With giggles and doubts like a whimsical dance,
I'll stumble my way right into romance.

The Illusion of Clarity

Once upon a time, I sought the truth,
Thinking clarity came with the wisdom of youth.
But it slipped through my fingers like fine sand,
Had me questioning if I'd misunderstood the plan.

Chasing illusions like butterflies in flight,
Each one I catch feels slightly off-white.
With fingers sticky from all this desire,
I ask if the answers are stuck in the mire.

In the haze of insight, I lose my way,
Thinking the fog might just be a play.
Witty remarks rain like a comic parade,
As clarity winks and starts to fade.

So let's flip the script and dance with the blind,
Savoring moments, whatever we find.
In this bright mess of whims and delight,
Mistakes wear crowns in the soft fading light.

Ripples of Contemplation

Why is the sky so blue, I ponder,
Does it cover up the thunder?
Why do socks disappear in the wash?
Is it because they want to frosh?

If cats could talk, what would they say?
Would they complain or just play?
Do plants feel sad when we leave?
Or do they just laugh, well, I believe!

Why do we trip over our own feet?
Is it the ground's way to cheat?
What's with the price of gas today?
Maybe I'll just roll away!

So many thoughts, like bubbles in air,
Floating around without a care.
Yet in this chaos, I find some cheer,
Maybe questions make the world near.

Embracing the Confusion

Why do we park in a drive-thru?
Is it just to confuse you?
What's the secret to a perfect pie?
Does it involve a well-timed lie?

Why do dogs chase after their tails?
Is it because their humor prevails?
Do fish think the ocean's a pool?
Or are they the ones who swim cool?

What does it mean when you feel lost?
Might it just be curiosity's cost?
Why do we find joy in silly memes?
Are they just whispers of our dreams?

Embracing chaos with a laugh so free,
Maybe confusion just wants to be!
With questions flying all around,
Perhaps the answers will be found.

When Choice Becomes a Maze

Chocolate or vanilla, such a hard pick,
What if I choose both? Oh, what a trick!
Should I wear the red or the blue shoe?
Watch, I'll regret whatever I do!

Do I sip coffee or stick to tea?
One gives energy, the other glee!
Salad or pizza for lunch today?
Why does this meal feel like a ballet?

Where do all these paths intertwine?
Choices like threads, forever divine!
What if I choose the wrong way again?
Will I end up lost in confusion's den?

In every turn, a laugh or a sigh,
Maybe each choice is a reason to fly!
With every decision shaping my fate,
I'll just keep dancing and call it great!

Tethered to Questions

Why do we always look for signs?
Is it because we're drawn like lines?
What if our dreams just play tricks?
Will we ever solve these bizarre mix?

Do squirrels have a master plan?
Or just chasing acorns—such a fan!
Can ducks really quack their thoughts?
Or is it just a game they've got?

Why do we fuss over tiny things?
Missing the joy that laughter brings?
What if worries were just balloons?
I'll let them float away with tunes!

Tethered to questions that float like kites,
Chasing them through days and nights.
With laughter as my trusty guide,
I'll sail through this curious tide!

In Search of Lost Certainties

Where did my keys go, oh what a quest,
The couch is a maze, my search is a test.
I check all my pockets, I check under beds,
Maybe I left them inside my own head.

Answers I seek, they swirl like a breeze,
In my tangled thoughts, I just can't find peace.
My sanity shrinks with each tick of the clock,
Was it the cat? Or the neighbor's pet rock?

Maps made of crumpled pizza boxes,
Guide me through life's ridiculous losses.
Yet when all's lost and I think I might cry,
My coffee's still there, and I'm ready to fly.

So here I remain with my humor intact,
In a world full of puzzles I surely attract.
With laughter as compass, I navigate mess,
For certainty's boring, I guess that's a plus!

Questions Knocking on My Door

Knock, knock, who's there? A question so sly,
It grins with a wink as it dances nearby.
I open the door, and what do I see?
A thought in a tux, sipping sweet tea.

"Why do we trip?" it inquires with glee,
"Is it just for the fun of a fall, can't you see?"
I ponder and chuckle, the answer eludes,
Perhaps it's a trick, just another ruse.

Next comes a query with a laugh and a shout,
"Why do you yell when you're lost in a crowd?"
I shrug my two shoulders, "It's just my way,
To make sure I'm heard through the chaos and fray!"

So I sit with these troubles, just take them in stride,
With questions as guests, I'll enjoy this ride.
They may not have answers, but they sure bring a grin,
At the party of thoughts where the laughter begins.

Expectation Meets Reality

I planned to be rich with a life full of craft,
But the universe chuckled—it just couldn't laugh.
With dreams made of dollars, I set out to grind,
Yet here I am munching on stale bits of rind.

"Expectations high!" I declared, filled with cheer,
"Reality's great, it's perfect, my dear!"
But as I step forward, oh what do I find?
A pile of laundry that's mocking my mind.

I thought I would soar with a star-studded fate,
But each time I dive, I just land on a plate.
With crumbs on my face and a smile that's wide,
I find there's great joy in an accidental ride.

So let's raise a toast to the dreams that we chase,
With giggles and stumbles, we welcome the race.
For every tall tower that sways in the breeze,
Is a lesson in laughter wrapped up in our cheese!

Curiosity's Tangled Web

A question unfolds like a spider's fine thread,
Weaving its way through each thought in my head.
"Why's the sky blue?" I ask the tall tree,
It shrugs its green leaves, "It's a mystery to me!"

"What makes a cat purr?" I ponder, perplexed,
She looks up at me, her tail is perplexed.
In a world full of wonders, I shrug with delight,
We giggle at answers that quickens the night.

"Does toast really land butter-side down?" I inquire,
As crumbs fall around like burnt little pyre.
The toast grins back, a cheeky little toast,
"Depends on the spirit—I'm buttered the most!"

So here I remain, a curious soul,
With tangled up thoughts that loop in a stroll.
The questions keep coming, and with them—some fun,
In this wacky web of wonder, I've only begun!

Contradictions in Bloom

In the garden of my mind, things twist,
A flower blooms, then heads to the mist.
I say 'yes' to tasks while needing a nap,
And run from the truth, oh what a mishap.

I bake cakes for breakfast, then munch on a shoe,
My dog thinks my diet is simply untrue.
With every decision, a fork in the road,
I dance in confusion, a curious code.

My plans are like jelly, they wobble and sway,
Tomorrow's ambitions just shuffle away.
I learn from my blunders, but what do I gain?
A humor-filled life, that's perfectly insane!

So here's to the chaos, the fun and the grind,
A world full of laughter, absurd and unkind.
My path might be crooked, but the joy never fades,
In contradictions blooming, where craziness raids.

Scribbles of the Heart

I've got a diary filled with doodles and dreams,
Where logic is missing, it's bursting at seams.
I scribble solutions that never make sense,
My heart's a clown's act, all crazy suspense.

I chased after fortune, but tripped on a dime,
The riches I sought were lost in my rhyme.
My heart's a comedian, cracking a joke,
While sanity's taking a stroll in the smoke.

Seeking sweet romance in a pile of to-do's,
I ask for advice from my cat with his blues.
Each scribble of love is a riddle, a tease,
For every answer leads to more mysteries, please!

So here's to the laughter, the joy in the mess,
With every blank page, I know I'll confess.
These scribbles may guide me, or lead me astray,
But I'll laugh at the what-ifs, come what may.

The Quest for Something More

I set out to find what that something could be,
A treasure of wisdom, perhaps a black tea.
But on my great journey, I lost my right sock,
The map was a riddle, a time-wasting clock.

I asked a wise owl for answers profound,
He hooted some nonsense and turned all around.
My compass was spinning, my heart felt so sore,
Yet I danced with a chicken, what more could it score?

The more that I seek, the fuzzier it seems,
I question my questions, unraveling dreams.
Hiding in humor, I wave my white flag,
With popcorn for insight and laughter to brag.

So here's to the quest, with its baffling bends,
Where not knowing stuff is what really transcends.
In seeking the unknown, my heart starts to soar,
Perhaps what I wanted was less, not more.

Chasing Elusive Truths

I tried to catch wisdom in a shimmering net,
But wisdom is slippery, a slippery pet.
I cornered it once, but it threw me a curve,
With answers like jelly, they wobble and swerve.

I asked silly questions, the answers were sly,
A goat told me truths with a wink of his eye.
I pondered at signs, a fortune-teller's booth,
But she just played darts with my challenging truth.

Every time I'm sure, uncertainty shouts,
It's played hide and seek, through odd twists and doubts.
I search for the meaning beneath all the jokes,
But laughter erupts while my wisdom just chokes.

In chasing elusive, with farcical glee,
I dance with the riddles, embracing the spree.
For the more that I question, the more I will find,
That the quest for clear answers is a laugh of a kind.

Reflections in a Broken Mirror

I looked at my face, what a sight!
A reflection that gave me a fright.
With hair standing up in rebellion,
I wondered if this was a wrong decision.

What's life without a splash of mischief?
I laughed at my hair, oh what a gift.
Every strand telling tales of the day,
Of the choices I made in a silly old way.

Should I eat that cake or three?
Calories don't count, can't you see?
The mirror sighed, 'You'll regret this!'
But my sweet tooth drowned out all the bliss.

So here's to the moments that cause a quake,
The big blunders and that last piece of cake.
When asking for wisdom, I find I'm a fool,
But my laughter's a treasure, that's my golden rule.

The Fragile Scale of Truth

On a scale of one to ten, where do I stand?
With truth in a balance, I sip from the can.
"I promise I'll exercise, give it a whirl!"
But the couch is so comfy, with snacks all a-furl.

The scale shakes, my weight starts to rise,
As I ponder the wisdom in calorie lies.
"Just one more slice," I confidently say,
While dodging my dreams that float far away.

I asked a wise friend for advice on this mess,
He shrugged, "Just be happy, not more or less."
So I sit with my chips and my pint of regret,
And declare that this balance is perfect—don't fret.

In the end, dear friends, when truths begin to blur,
Remember that laughter can certainly stir,
The scale may be fragile, but here's the best part:
Joy comes from the snacks, that are hitched to the heart.

Confessions of a Wandering Mind

My thoughts are like squirrels, they dart and they weave,
In a forest of confusion, hard to believe.
I tell myself, focus! But then I get lost,
Chasing a notion that comes at a cost.

Did I lock the door? Or was it the fridge?
My mind wanders far, like a bird on a ridge.
With every distraction, my tasks fall apart,
Each question I ask feels like a crazy dart.

I'm supposed to be writing, or maybe I'm not?
Oh look, a cat! Wait, what was I sought?
As I ponder the meaning of why does this swirl,
I lose all the sense, just a curious girl.

But maybe this wandering, this dance in my head,
Is where all the fun and adventure are fed.
So here's to the chaos, the noise of my mind,
I cherish the laughter that's often unlined.

The Art of Missing the Mark

I set out to bake a cake, as grand as can be,
But the flour exploded; oh, what a spree!
With icing like glue, and candles askew,
My masterpiece looked like it belonged in a zoo.

Instructions were simple, or so it seemed,\nThen I mixed
in some salt, thinking it's whipped cream.
The oven roared back, "What have you made?"
A confection of chaos, a sweet charade.

I tried to impress with a poem for you,
But rhymes went astray, and nonsense just grew.
Each line like a punchline, a deliberate miss,
In the art of confusion, I find my own bliss.

So here's to mishaps, the charm and the glee,
To the cakes that don't rise, and the poems like me.
For in every disaster, a chuckle does spark,
In the canvas of folly, I'm leaving my mark.

Paradoxes Beneath the Surface

Why do we park on driveways,
And yet we drive on parkways?
The more I learn, the less I know,
Like a balloon that steals the show.

I tried to swim but only sank,
In my own logic, that's a prank.
With tangled thoughts in the mix,
Was that a joke or just a fix?

I questioned socks that go unpaired,
Like pairs of shoes that felt impaired.
The world's an upside-down delight,
Who knew confusion could be bright?

Yet here I stand, with questions undone,
With answers that seem like a pun.
Embrace the silly in the day,
For wisdom, sometimes, likes to play.

Existential Puzzles

Why do I snooze my morning calls,
While chasing thoughts that bounce like balls?
A riddle wrapped in a cloak of doubt,
I shout answers when I'm not quite out.

Coffee tastes like a bold critique,
On dreams I had, it takes a peek.
If I'm awake, why am I lost?
These ponderings, they come at a cost.

Up is down, and left is right,
I made a plan, but lost the fight.
Every 'yes' hits me like a wall,
And somehow, no one hears my call.

Yet in this maze, I find my cheer,
With every twist, I persevere.
Laughing at life's quirky charade,
I'll dance through puzzles the world has made.

The Art of Misinterpretation

I hear 'sit' and I leap and twirl,
Was that a dance or a funny whirl?
A recipe for disaster, indeed,
Where I'm the chef, but lost the need.

I guessed the plot, but turned the page,
What a story of foolish rage!
Trying to paint with colors gray,
Why do I brighten the dullest day?

Diagnostics call for clear intent,
But my signs often get misread, I vent.
My jokes, like boomerangs, come back,
And leave me wobbling on this track.

So here's to blunders that come my way,
With laughter loud, I'll seize the day.
For in my folly, there's something grand,
A canvas of chaos, unplanned and unbanned.

Searching for Solid Ground

I stumbled upon a stone of thought,
But logic fled, and wisdom fought.
With every step, the earth did shake,
Why is it real? Could this be fake?

Can solid ground be a swirling maze?
With answers hidden in the haze.
Where clocks tick slowly, and time's astray,
What do we do when lost in play?

I sought the truth beneath a rug,
But pulled it back, and there was a bug.
The more I searched for what is right,
The funnier things became, quite a sight!

So here's my quest, haphazard, odd,
In laughter, I find my own God.
For every wobble on this path,
There's joy in questions and misplaced math.

Threads of Disarray

In the morning light, I seek the right path,
But my GPS just laughs, what a twist of math.
I tie my shoelaces, one's taking a break,
As I trip on my thoughts, for goodness' sake!

Brewed a cup of coffee, forgot the beans,
I poured in the blank, what in the scenes?
Each step is a riddle, I can't crack it well,
Like finding my way in a carnival spell.

The dog stole my sandwich, now he's the king,
While I'm in the corner contemplating my bling.
Is it the crumbs I chase, or my dignity's face?
A tango with chaos, a dance with no grace.

As the evening sets in, I ponder my day,
Did I mean to offend the cat in this play?
With questions aplenty, I shrug and just grin,
For at least I know where the chaos begins!

The Harmony of Questions

Why is the sky blue? I ponder and muse,
Yet find it more fun to just sing the blues.
What if the moon made a phone call, it's true?
Would it dial up the stars, or just me and you?

I asked the wise owl where wisdom abounds,
He hooted and flew, pushing me round.
With each curious thought, a new giggle is found,
As I chase my thoughts, I tumble to the ground.

What if all the socks conspire to run?
Would they hide in the dryer, just having some fun?
I'll search every corner, I'll laugh to the core,
Yet find I have questions and still need some more.

In a parade of queries, I twirl for a while,
With a fumble and stumble, I'm teaching my style.
Each guess a surprise, each answer a game,
In the symphony of questions, I'll never be the same!

Trails of Unfinished Thoughts

I set out to write a profound little note,
But my mind is a boat with a missing coat.
Drifting through ideas, like leaves in the breeze,
Caught in translation, oh will someone please!

My pen dances wildly, but can't find its beat,
Like blending spaghetti and chocolate to eat.
Every thought I uncover seems just out of reach,
A classroom of echoes, but no one to teach.

A trail of confusion, I'll follow it still,
Hoping one day it'll lead to some thrill.
With questions like candy, I munch with a grin,
Yet all I have left is a twist of the spin.

So I scribble in circles, a riddle of sorts,
My missteps become laughter, a series of sports.
In trails of unfinished thoughts, I shall roam,
With every confusion, I'm still feeling at home!

What Lies Beneath My Decisions

I flipped a coin for a choice, such a risk,
It landed on 'oops,' what a twist in the brisk.
Should I eat that last slice? Oh, what a scene,
But the fridge holds a council, and it's quite mean.

Decisions like puzzles, all jumbled and tossed,
Choosing between pandas, or whatever's lost.
I ponder my fate while tripping on chairs,
These choices I make, do they lead anywhere?

Like wearing two mismatched socks on a spree,
I strive for perfection, how hard can it be?
With each rogue decision, a laugh fills the air,
A carnival of mishaps, chaos laid bare.

So I dance with my choices, a clumsy ballet,
Each step is a question, come learn how I sway.
What lies beneath is just laughter and fun,
For every wrong turn, there's a new pun begun!

The Tug of Uncertainty

In the game of what should I do,
My compass spins, it's all askew.
Should I dance? Or should I eat?
My choices seem to taste like feet.

Should I jump? Should I sit tight?
My thoughts fly left, they take to flight.
With every change, a funny twist,
I laugh, I grin, I can't resist.

Donuts call me, so do the frights,
Should I binge or break all rights?
A jester's hat upon my crown,
In this circus, I'll not frown.

So tightrope walk on doubts I'll glide,
With juggling acts my joy won't hide.
For every stumble, there's a cheer,
In this funny game, I persevere.

Inquiries on a Broken Path

Down the path of blunders bright,
I trip on answers, lose my sight.
Should I laugh or should I cry?
The squirrels seem to wonder why.

I asked a tree for wisdom grand,
It just shrugged and drew in sand.
Can I trust the winds that sway?
They only giggle, drift away.

With every turn, my choices fade,
Like a game where I misplayed.
So here I dance, with sprained intent,
And wonder where my time was spent.

Oh, fateful steps, you steal my shoes,
In this riddle, there's no excuse.
But let me prance with split ends bold,
In my foolish heart, I'll find gold.

The Spectrum of Regret

Behind each veil of silly slips,
Resides a treasure of comic quips.
Was that a chance, or just a sneeze?
I'll let you guess, while I munch cheese.

In colors bright, my hopes collide,
With shades of "oops!" I wear with pride.
Should I have asked? Or just said "no"?
When answers dance like a freak show.

Regrets parade with faces wide,
Each one winks like it's joyride.
I learned to juggle my misfit dreams,
Through every laugh, it surely seems.

So here I stand, a fool with zest,
For every stumble, I'm truly blessed.
In this quirky mess, I have grown,
With laughter loud, I've found my throne.

Musings from a Torn Page

In scribbles wide, I chase my fate,
With crumpled thoughts that can't wait.
Should I leap from clouds above?
Or sip some tea with a grumpy dove?

The pen I wield has quirks of plight,
It jots down the nonsense of day and night.
I asked a cat, "What's wisdom dear?"
It blinked and yawned, "Just grab a beer."

Between the lines, the mishaps churn,
With every scratch, there's so much to learn.
Is this a tale, or merely a farce?
With every laugh, it's quite a blast!

So here I am on this torn page spree,
Crafting nonsense, oh so free.
With playful pen, I'll try, I'll fail,
In this merry tale of life's grand trail.

The Weight of Unsaid Words

I ponder in silence, my thoughts a parade,
Each unspoken word, a grand charade.
The cat stares at me, judging my plight,
As I trip through the jargon that dances at night.

My friend asked for wisdom, I offered a pun,
But he rolled his eyes like it's all just for fun.
In the awkwardness blossomed a bouquet of dread,
As I sat there wondering, 'What's stuck in my head?'

Should I speak up and risk making things worse?
Or let the air linger, an unspoken curse?
Once I thought wisdom was just like a chart,
Turns out it's a jigsaw, missing a part.

So on I shall wander, through thoughts that I keep,
With my companion, that cat, who's now fast asleep.
In this silent devotion, I'll forge an old pact,
To find all the words that I've quietly lacked.

Paths to Nowhere

I set off in the morning, with plans in my heart,
But somehow ended up in a pie shop's part.
"Is the pie really good?" asked a swell in the line,
I chuckled and nodded, 'It's simply divine!'

My map told me places; my gut took a break,
While I wandered in circles, unsure what to make.
With each step I took, I felt quite the fool,
'Where am I?' I pondered, 'Is this even a school?'

I found a nice café, and thought, 'What the heck?'
To forget all my failures and just eat a speck.
The barista, amused, served coffee with flair,
As I tried to explain how I ending up there.

But paths left untraveled can lead you to pie,
With giggles and laughter as time slips on by.
Maybe lost is the new found, a quest without end,
And in all of my wandering, new flavors will blend.

Sifting Through the Ashes of What Was

I once dreamt of greatness, or so I believed,
But I find in the rubble, the dreams I deceived.
With ashes of plans drifting high up in smoke,
Each flicker of failure could make a good joke.

I sift through the remnants; is that my old shoe?
What kind of disaster? Oh, where were the screws?
It seems I built castles on paper-thin sand,
Counted my blessings while frowning, unplanned.

"Just try to be smarter," my mentor would say,
Yet here I sit chuckling at all I let stray.
I'd crown myself king of the flop and the fail,
In the treasure of blunders, I'm sure to prevail.

So raise up a glass filled with pie crusts and dreams,
Cheers to the chaos and jumbled up schemes.
For in every disaster, there's laughter to find,
In the ashes of what was, we're all intertwined.

A Mind Full of Misdirection

My brain seems to wander; it's lost in a maze,
A tumble of thoughts that just enter a daze.
While I seek out the answers, they giggle and flee,
Turning all of my logic into a potpourri.

I stumbled through riddles, like a fool with no clue,
Who thought pondering hard means I'd find something new.
"Where'd you leave the keys?" yelled a voice from the hall,
I searched for a moment, then tripped on the wall.

I advised my dear friend to always stand tall,
But my feet seemed to dance as I swayed and would fall.
"Just hold onto reason!" I yelled with a grin,
As the cat once again found a way to break in.

So here's to confusion, the jester on stage,
With a mind full of quirks trapped inside this old cage.
In each twist and turn, misdirection is fun,
For laughter defines the journey I've spun.

www.ingramcontent.com/pod-product-compliance
Lightning Source LLC
Chambersburg PA
CBHW071818160426
43209CB00003B/127